Living with a Narcissist: Finding Strength and Renewal in Relationships

Barbara J. Harris

Introduction

Narcissism is a term you've certainly heard used frequently in psychological contexts. The concept of narcissism encompasses several DSM diagnoses, including Narcissist Personality Disorder, Borderline Personality Disorder, Oppositional Defiant Disorder, and others.

I'm doing this because the current psychological field is struggling with defining mental illness beyond identifying its symptoms.

In this post, I will define narcissism and mental health in terms that many professionals in the mental health field would avoid because discussing feelings is considered a scientific taboo. I'm doing this because the mental health issues we face today are too significant to "wait and see," and we need to take decisive action to define, test, and heal them. A society of narcissists, like a society of cripples, can never hope to prosper or endure.

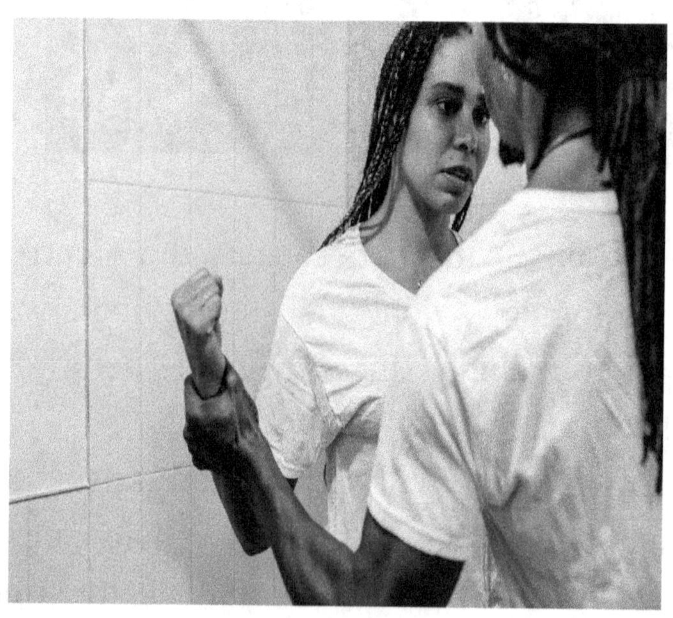

The Narcissism Self Esteem Gap

Narcissism is the inverse of self esteem.

A psychologically healthy individual is fully aware and appreciative of their entire emotional range, whereas a narcissist is utterly clueless or contemptuous of their emotions.

Most people have a complex blend of these two extremes, with an internal inventory of "safe" and "unsafe" emotions to express and acknowledge in their thinking. In contrast to the entries on self esteem, this article provides an overview of the critical characteristics of narcissism.

It's all about self-esteem, and having none.

The inability to regard one's own personal feelings, beliefs, and desires as having any fundamental value is at the heart of narcissism. If you are from a mainstream field of psychology, you might think I have it backwards because the DSM definition of narcissism emphasizes that they have little empathy or sympathy for others. I'm going to take a risk and suggest that conventional psychology is incorrect on this topic.

Narcissists have empathy and the ability to profoundly care about other people and especially animals; however, they lack the ability to relate to themselves as having any fundamental worth.

What is important to understand is that narcissists are aware of other people's sentiments; they simply do not value other people's feelings. Similarly, narcissists do not consider their own sentiments to be valuable.

The brain is a complex organ, but consider our emotions to be a kind of sixth sense (much like seeing and hearing), but they tell us about what we value. So when we look at ice cream, money, or a buddy, our "value/feeling complex" informs us that we appreciate them; similarly, when we look at other people or ourselves, the same "value/feeling complex" is at work.

When a narcissist looks at other people, they only see their physical or financial worth; they are unable to see their inherent or spiritual worth. When people look in the mirror, they only see their physical worth, not their inherent or spiritual worth. Thus, even if they are physically appealing and are aware of it, a narcissist perceives their emotional/spiritual self as completely worthless, just as other people do.

It is commonly stated that narcissists see other people as mere objects on the landscape; this is correct; however, they also see themselves as mere objects, which hurts them more than it hurts other people; you cannot see their hurt because they do not know how to express or deal with their own hurt. Simply cover it up, or pretend to be harmed in order to claim victimhood.

Because narcissists are utterly disconnected from their feelings, everything they do is for the benefit of others.

They act as others expect them to act, speak as others expect them to speak, and adapt their interests and life goals to meet the expectations of their family, friends, and partner. Although they are ambitious, cutthroat, and frequently draw a lot of attention to themselves, they do these things to meet the expectations that they believe others have of them.

Thus, from the narcissist's point of view, they devote their entire lives to other people and find it perplexing and terrible when others abuse and reject them. As Selfish as you would imagine a narcissist is, calling them that would actually perplex them if they could express it.

The narcissist's issues originate from the fact that, while they may not respect their own emotions, this does not mean they are emotionless. Under the calm and calculated veneer of the narcissist is the complete spectrum of emotions that any other person experiences; they merely ignore them as best as they can since they consider their feelings to be unimportant.

Because narcissists ignore their own emotional needs in favor of fulfilling the needs and desires of others, they are usually a whirlwind of rage, disappointments, resentments, hate, and anxieties on the inside. Different types of narcissists employ various tactics for concealing or rationalizing their mental torments. They are, nevertheless, all terribly confused and disordered people on the inside.

When a narcissist begins to take their feelings seriously and begins to respond to their emotional needs by being accountable for their emotions and taking care of the reasons causing their misery, the narcissism vanishes and they become mentally healthy.

In principle, this process is straightforward, but in fact it is lengthy, perplexing, and painful. Specifically, a narcissist will avoid paying attention to their emotions since the first feelings they will encounter will be extreme agony, and it is totally reasonable to seek to avoid discomfort. A narcissist will gain significantly by having a deep connection with someone they trust; yet, this is extremely difficult, especially if the narcissist has been severely mistreated.

Love? Relationships, on the other hand, are about power...

Even if a narcissist ignores their own feelings, they still require love, understanding, and friendship, as well as someone to pay attention to them in order to compensate for the fact that they ignore themselves. We shall perish as humans without these things because they provide us with a sense of worth, and life is absolutely meaningless and terrible without a sense of worth.

As a result, narcissists will continue to seek out relationships. Being out of touch with their feelings, on the other hand, implies they will choose a spouse who will impress others: physically handsome, wealthy, popular, talented, bright, and so on...

whatever attributes they believe their friends and family value the most. Again, they choose acquaintances and lovers to impress others rather than to satisfy their own inner desires.

Love, on the other hand, is founded on closeness, and intimacy is formed on the ability to openly communicate emotions with someone. Sharing, being heard, and listening to another person share these behaviors foster trust, closeness, and a healthy relationship. How does a person who is emotionally disconnected, form and maintain an intimate relationship? The simple answer is that they cannot.

Instead, narcissists would act out and simulate false emotions to fool another person into falling in love with them or becoming (physically/emotionally) intimate with them. However, because the connection is usually improper and/or the narcissist is utterly dishonest, the narcissist cannot be trusted.

They know the relationship is a sham, they know they are a sham, and they know that if their partner discovers the truth, the relationship would end, thus they do not trust the individuals with whom they are intimate. One cannot trust someone who is deceiving them; if they trusted them, they would not be deceiving them.

However, there can be no love without mutual trust: only a power struggle. Because narcissists desire deep relationships, the other person possesses what the narcissist sorely requires: a sense of value. This reliance on another person to provide the elixir of life, when they may just as easily walk away, makes narcissists feel powerless at the start of a relationship.

Thus, a narcissist will try to accelerate the connection as soon as possible in order to feel confident with their partner's interest in the narcissist: this is commonly done by freely giving sex, money, and expressions of endearment in order to boost the other person's attachment rapidly. This is in addition to changing their ideals and desires to match those of their spouse.

In the early phases of any relationship (friendship or love), narcissists are empathic and caring because when a person feels weak, they are more sensitive to other people's emotions. However, as the narcissist gets confidence that the other person has taken them into their confidence or has become dependent on them (narcissists are drawn to other narcissists), the narcissist's sensitivity and compassion fade.

In a relationship controlled by operant conditioning, the narcissist's compassion is proportional to how powerful they feel in the relationship, therefore individuals tend to figure this out and begin lashing out at the narcissist.

As a result, the narcissist's relationships become continual power battles, with each side attempting to overpower the other, in order to acquire the empathy they seek so desperately from a powerless friend/spouse.

Having another person's empathy is practically the same as having another person's devotion, which helps a narcissist feel worthwhile. Thus, a narcissist will deprive a person of their sense of self-worth in order to make them obedient to them, and the other person will feel hurt and abandoned if they have the self-respect to leave or resist being gutted.

As a result, a close relationship with a narcissist will almost certainly end in abuse. It could even escalate into physical violence and threats. If you're in a relationship with a narcissist, the only safe option is to end it. If you try to deal with them by not responding to their provocations, they will either beat you down, escalate their abuse, or abandon you.

You cannot argue with a complete narcissist because to reason with someone, that person must regard your thoughts and wishes.

If they are only moderately narcissistic, there may be some opportunity for maneuvering by applauding them for their moments of clarity, honesty, and fairness, but keep in mind that if they are severely narcissistic, they can be extremely manipulating.

Remember that your safety is the most crucial thing; narcissists are masters at hurting others while manipulating perceptions to make themselves appear to be the victim; in reality, they probably actually feel like the victim underneath it all.

They've been known to encourage others into attacking them, then exploit the victim's credibility to completely demolish their "attacker." You will never win a power battle with a narcissist unless you become the worst narcissist you can be. It's not worth it; leave the relationship to protect yourself.

Identifying a Narcissist

Because narcissists are disconnected from their emotions and do not respect their personal ideas and desires, they can be easily identified by interrogating them about their thoughts, feelings, and desires. Narcissists will usually have a cover story for these inquiries that makes them look to be in control of their own feelings, thoughts, and desires. They learn this through experience, and narcissists frequently pretend to improve by becoming better liars. If you are attentive and persistent in investigating their sentiments, you will eventually reach a point where they snap at you and withdraw as if they are experiencing an anxiety attack. This is due to an anxiety attack (explaining how this works would take a complete essay in and of itself).

The use of deception and guilt trips is another approach to identify a narcissist. Because narcissists lack internal values, they are great moral relativists and apply a double standard in every case. A double standard that always results in them winning while you lose.

Indeed, there is no such thing as a win-win situation in the narcissist's world; everything is a win-lose situation. A narcissist must be able to understand their own sentiments enough to have personal values and integrity in order to comprehend a win-win solution. They may claim to have high moral standards, but this is all talk and no substance: when a person violates their own moral code, intense inner pain always results (except in cases of sociopathy, which is caused by a series of very rare brain defects), so a person with high self-esteem will take his pain seriously and do something to make reparations, whereas a narcissist will not take his pain seriously and will feel no compulsion to respond to it.

Aside from that, narcissists are often gorgeous, rich, and/or charming people, simply because others are less patient with their manipulations and guilt trips if they are not attractive and appealing. When manipulation and deception no longer work for a narcissist, he or she will either try to solve their problems, seek treatment, or commit suicide. Because gorgeous, wealthy, and charming people will always have a consistent supply of people eager to be too pleasant to them, they are the most likely to maintain severe narcissism throughout adulthood.

This is also why narcissists are so difficult to treat. When their physical beauty fades, they run out of money, or they run out of people willing to put up with their falsehoods and double standards, narcissists typically recover.

Some Closing Thoughts

Narcissists will severely abuse and neglect their children as parents. They will regard their children as property to be exploited and managed in their favor. Abuse at the hands of a narcissist parent guarantees that their children will be narcissists as well, unless there is someone in the child's life who can model positive self-esteem for them.

Remember that if you're in a relationship with a narcissist, it's most likely because your behavior is supporting them; you may not be entirely narcissistic, but you almost surely have some narcissistic qualities that need to be addressed. Most of the time, depriving a narcissist of attention and resources until they make a decision for themselves to get better is the only genuine cure, and tragically, very frequently all you can do is avoid them and warn others of their behavior.

Teenage girls with narcissism will frequently prostitute their bodies to gain attention and resources from others, and they can do so because they don't care how bad it makes them feel, and there is no shortage of people willing to enable this type of behavior from them.

Finally,
narcissism is the most devastating mental condition a human being can suffer from, especially in its most severe manifestations. When provoked, they are self-destructive, irresponsible, cruel, and even homicidal.

They instigate workplace conflicts and tensions, shirk accountability, seek authority, and leave a trail of ruin in their aftermath. While at the same time appearing to be the victim. Adult narcissism is particularly difficult to treat since adults have the freedom to leave therapy at any time, and forcing a narcissist to attend therapy would just traumatize them further.

The best way to prevent narcissism is to demonstrate healthy and self-loving behaviors to children while they are young. Though modeling such excellent behaviors to kids at any age would be vicariously healing for them.

Even if both of a child's parents are narcissists, teachers and relatives with strong self-esteem can give them a second chance by lessening the intensity, increasing their chances of learning how to cure themselves as adults. Remember that one does not teach self-esteem; rather, one lives it and inspires others to do the same.

Chapter 1

A summary of relationship concerns

Relationships with our loved ones, whether romantic and platonic, bring us immense joy, significance, and a sense of understanding and connection. Every partnership experiences difficulties at some point, ranging from squabbles to intimacy issues and financial difficulties.

Conflict is normal in relationships, and it can even help us grow and connect. A complete lack of disagreement is frequently a red flag that partners are disengaged.

Relationship troubles can, in certain situations, trigger symptoms of common mental health conditions such as anxiety disorders and depressive disorders. Relationship difficulties can sometimes result in emotional or physical abuse. When relationship problems become regular or serious, they can disrupt our everyday life. Relationship difficulties are difficult to quantify since they vary so greatly. Recent research studies, however, indicate that relationship issues are common, particularly in romantic partnerships.

In the United States, intimate relationship violence, including physical and emotional abuse, is also relatively widespread. Over 10 Million American adults are victims of intimate partner violence each year, according to the National Coalition Against Domestic Violence.

Relationship Issues Symptoms
Relationship problems are unique to each individual, and psychological and emotional responses to relationship challenges

fluctuate greatly. Some of the most prevalent signs of a relationship problem are:

Excessive anxiety or worry

You may be preoccupied with relationship problems or have anxiety symptoms. Feelings of fear and dread, shortness of breath, heart palpitations, nervousness, rapid heartbeat, chest pain, dizziness, panic attacks, dry mouth, sleeplessness, and nausea are some of the physical symptoms of anxiety.

Sadness or depression

Depending on how serious your relationship problems are, you may have a depressed mood, a major depressive episode, or other depression symptoms.

A loss of interest in daily activities, exhaustion, restlessness, changes in appetite, feelings of hopelessness, and gloomy thoughts are some of the symptoms of depression.

High stress levels

You may feel overwhelmed or suffer from physical stress symptoms such as muscle tightness, chronic pain, headaches, sleep issues, and digestive problems. High cortisol levels can cause long-term health issues and medical diseases like weight gain, high blood pressure, heart disease, and even heart attack and stroke.

Conflicts with friends and family members

If you're experiencing relationship difficulties, you may notice that other conflicts with friends, family members, or loved ones occur as a result of resentment or impatience.

Insecurity in your relationship can lead to emotions of worthlessness and self-esteem difficulties.

Relationship Problem Types

Relationship troubles are deeply personal and vary greatly. Some of the most common types of relationship issues are:

Infidelity/trust issues: You may wonder if your spouse is being truthful about your relationship or other elements of your life.

Arguments over tasks and raising children are typical in the home.

Communication problems might emerge when you or your spouse do not feel heard or understood.

Finances are among the top stressors in romantic relationships, according to a 2015 national poll conducted by the American Psychological Association (APA).

Priority issues: Relationship conflicts frequently emerge as a result of issues with attention and preferences, particularly when making crucial decisions.

Issues with sex and intimacy: Differing sex urges, as well as doubts about attraction and fulfillment, can lead to intimacy problems.

Major life changes, like the birth of a child, moving, a stressful incident, or menopause, can all lead to relationship breakdowns.

Violence and abuse: When a relationship is characterized by power and control, it is most likely abusive. According to The National Center on Domestic Violence, Trauma, and Mental Health, there are also strong correlations between substance use and intimate partner violence.

Substance abuse can range from alcohol to illegal narcotics and amphetamines.

What should you do if you're having relationship problems?
It is critical to get treatment if you are facing stress, disagreement, or danger in a relationship, regardless of the severity.

Among the therapy options are:

Therapy: Working with a mental health expert can help you address and resolve relationship concerns. You can go to talk therapy on your own, or you and your partner can go to couples or family therapy together.

When you're having relationship problems, it can be helpful to reach out to other key individuals in your life for assistance.

Opening up to close family members or a trusted friend might modify your perception and remind you that you have other people who love and rely on you. Consider asking loved ones for a safe place to stay if you are experiencing violence.

Self-care: If you have chronic stress, a bad mood, or a lot of anxiety, self-care can help you take care of your mental and physical health. Avoiding coffee, eating a well-balanced diet, making time for regular exercise, getting adequate sleep, and discovering new interests can all help to improve your mood and alleviate your symptoms.

Medications: If you have anxiety or depression symptoms, your doctor may recommend antidepressants, benzodiazepines, selective serotonin reuptake inhibitors (SSRIs), beta-blockers, or anti-anxiety medication to help you feel better and function better in everyday life, according to the Anxiety and Depression Association of America.

While drugs may have negative effects, consulting with a psychiatrist can help you select the best treatment option for you.

Choosing the Best Therapist

Therapy is the first step toward healing your relationship, whether you're facing new issues in your partnership or struggling to heal after a severe life event. Therapists use several types of psychotherapy, or talk therapy, to assist in the resolution of relationship issues, such as:

Psychodynamic psychotherapy: Psychodynamic psychotherapy explores maladaptive coping strategies and relational patterns through self-reflection and self-examination. Psychodynamic therapy is an effective treatment for assisting patients in navigating traumatic situations such as childhood abuse, neglect, sexual assault, and other traumatic events that may lead to relationship problems.

Cognitive-behavioral therapy (CBT): A type of talk therapy, CBT helps couples address the beliefs and behaviors that lead to relationship problems and helps them see their problems in a new light.

According to the National Institutes of Mental Health (NIMH), CBT is effective in treating a wide range of mental health conditions, including bipolar disorder, post-traumatic stress disorder (PTSD), substance misuse, ADHD, and major depressive disorder.

Interpersonal therapy (IPT): is a type of psychotherapy that tries to strengthen interpersonal relationships and social interactions in order to lessen distress. IPT can help with clinical depression, persistent depressive disorder, and postpartum depression, as well as anxiety disorders like agoraphobia, social anxiety disorder, obsessive-compulsive disorder (OCD), panic disorder, generalized anxiety disorder (GAD), specific phobias, and separation anxiety disorder.

According to Harvard Medical School, relationships are essential to our pleasure and well-being. Relationships, on the other hand, require effort to preserve, especially amid the ongoing COVID-19 pandemic.

Reach out to a certified therapist through WithTherapy to find the proper psychologist, psychiatrist, social worker, marital and family therapist, or counselor for your mental health needs.

Regardless of your preferences or needs, they will match you with a mental health practitioner you can trust. One of the therapists on the WithTherapy platform will assist you in developing a treatment plan to improve communication, deal with relationship stressors, and strive toward a healthy relationship.

Chapter 2

understanding of the Narcissistic Abuser

understanding of narcissistic abuse In our culture today, the Narcissistic abuser has reached epidemic proportions (affecting both males and females), but few therapists (Psychotherapists, Counselors, Coaches, and Supervisors) would be quick to recognize it in the therapy room when clients present with what is now known as Narcissistic Victim Syndrome (NVS).

To effectively work with narcissistic victim abuse, the therapist must first grasp what narcissistic personality disorder (NPD) is, what causes it, and what the insidious behaviors look like. Failing to comprehend the very complicated narcissistic behavior entails failing to comprehend the psychological horror that your client has endured.

However, once understood, you will have the clarity of vision to shed light on the dysfunctional narcissistic behavior that has perplexed and befuddled your client for so long. Narcissistic behavior is so insidious that it keeps the victim living in a nightmare hell where they are constantly walking on eggshells to the point that their ability to function is impaired. To prevent needless repetition of "he/she" and "his/her" in this essay, I will use the pronoun "he" to describe NPD.

THE FOLLOWING INSIGHTS CAN HELP YOU UNDERSTAND NARCISSISTIC BEHAVIOR.

1. Rejection

The narcissist fears rejection more than anything else in the world because he is suffering from the core wounds of abandonment. Because of his profound wounds, his antenna is sensitive to any hint of imminent rejection (real or imagined), and he will go to any length to avoid the overwhelming sense of shame that it brings.

As a result, he constructs sophisticated defense mechanisms all around him, and he will lie, cheat, abuse, and manipulate in any way possible to protect his vulnerable false-self.

2. False-self

The Narcissist urgently desires love, yet he is scared of intimacy due to his excessive fear of abandonment, betrayal, and rejection, leaving him extremely lonely within himself. He lacks the ability to create good connections because he has never learned the art of honest communication. "himself" is the first loving and perfectly controlling object he bonds to.

He has become the object of his own desire, much like the mythical character Narcissus, and he projects that idealized image onto the world through a persona that is a False Self, a false self that he perceives as being omnipotent (all-powerful) and omniscience (all-knowing). Unfortunately, these visions are confabulations, intricate works of fiction with little or no resemblance to reality.

From there, he transforms others into things, removing all emotional risk. The "Sources of Narcissistic Supply" are these mental representations of relevant or significant persons.

3. Narcissistic Supply

Narcissistic Supply refers to persons who offer the narcissist with a steady source of attention, approbation, devotion, admiration, and so forth. The

attention they receive from the "Supply Source" is critical for the narcissist's survival; without it, they would perish (physically or symbolically), because their fragile ego relies on it to manage their unstable self-worth and self-esteem.

The narcissist believes they are incredibly self-sufficient. They couldn't deal with the idea that they needed someone, because needing someone carries the risk of rejection. This would imply a limit to their ability or that they are insufficient.

Furthermore, any indication of independence and autonomy from their "supply" enrages them. Because the narcissistic supply exists to serve them, they attempt to cement their source of supply into the position they have created for themselves, and thus remain under the narcissist's control. Any attempt by the supply guy to not comply enrages him.

4. fury

His narcissistic behavior is characterized by fury. The rage is the narcissist's method of yelling for attention because everything revolves around them, their demands, needs, and desires. Narcissistic rage is an uncontrollable and sudden outburst of anger caused by a narcissistic hurt.

Narcissistic injury is a danger to the self-esteem or worth of a narcissist. Rage has various shapes, but they all point to the same thing: "revenge." It is vital to note that narcissistic rage should not be mistaken with anger (although the two are similar); the narcissist's rage is not always triggered by a situation that would normally elicit anger in a person. Their wrath frightens people, and seeing others' terror makes the narcissist feel like they have won, making them feel even more powerful and in charge of the situation, which also satisfies their sadistic nature.

Their cognitive distortions, fragmentation, dissociation, stunted emotional development, black and white thinking, false self, grandiosity, desire for attention (even if negative), need to be right, and lack of empathy are all supported and covered up by their wrath. In short, the narcissist's "rage" contains the actions required for the narcissist to defend himself against his hostile world (i.e. splitting, devaluation, projection, projective identification, and so on), but these defenses, like a double-edged sword, make any closeness or intimacy impossible, whether intentionally or unintentionally.

However, the wrath makes him feel as if he is regaining control anytime he is afraid of losing it.

5. Power and Control

In his daily life, he strives to dominate each individual and group with whom he interacts, whether at home, at work, or at social events. His power is not "power with," but "power over" all he sees.

His position of power and control serves as a springboard for verbal and emotional abuse. For example, while he imposes financial constraints on his family, he is free to make spending decisions for himself. When it comes to the day-to-day care of the household, he does not participate in the menial activities, but he undermines and degrades those who do.

His energy is spent on "ideas" on how things should be done, while the actual doing is left to the "plebs" to perform the labor and ideas for him.

As the work is completed, the narcissist criticizes and complains, failing to offer credit where credit is due.

He convinces himself that it is his brains that direct the work, that nothing would be accomplished without him, and he completely fails to appreciate the work of others. He's lost in his own self-importance.

6. Grandiosity

The most noticeable and distinguishing symptom of people with Narcissistic

Personality Disorder is grandiosity. Grandiosity can manifest itself as an excessive over-valuation of one's talents and abilities, a fixation with fantasies of endless beauty, power, fortune, or success, and a belief in one's own unrealistic superiority and uniqueness. This is frequently followed by arrogant, pretentious, self-centered, and self-referential narcissistic behavior.

The research demonstrates that the grandiose narcissist exaggerates his talents, capacity, and achievements in an unrealistic fashion, He either believes in his invulnerability or fails to acknowledge his own limitations.

His grandiose ideas cause him to assume that he is not dependent on others. Needing others would fill him with immense guilt.

7. Shame

Shame appears to be the result of the narcissist's grandiosity and yearning for perfection. When a narcissist feels shame, he feels inadequate, imperfect, and inferior. He has narcissistically harmed himself, and he is now likely to explode in wrath because he feels prominent, exposed, and vulnerable to shame.

He is overcome with anxiety because he fears he will lose the imagined love and admiration of others if he isn't perfect. So, cognitively, the narcissist is pushed to do better and better inside the rigorous boundaries they have constructed for themselves; however, unconsciously, they are unable to regulate their behavior, so they and anybody around them must suffer.

8. Perfectionism

The narcissist's obsessional behavior, governed by a False Self, sets unreasonable goals. He then strives to keep those objectives alive in the midst of what he views to be an imperfect reality. This strain that the narcissist imposes on himself stems from his unyielding quest for perfection, which is required to preserve his grandiosity and delusion of omnipotence.

Furthermore, because the narcissist is dominated by his "black and white" or "all right or all wrong" thinking, he can only evaluate his accomplishments in one of two ways: as the greatest accomplishments, or as the biggest failures. There is no place for the creation of a process for future learning since there is no middle area.

So he either achieves his positive ego ideal (his Eureka moment), where he enjoys euphoric self-esteem to his liking, where he may feel a wonderful feeling of achievement and flaunt it to the world with pride, or he does not. Or he has a negative ego ideal in which his omnipotence is undermined, calling into doubt his sense of perfection and uniqueness.

When the latter occurs, the narcissist experiences feelings of shame, vulnerability, and failure; his pride of accomplishment is likely to be diminished, and his commitment and capacity to follow through on this achievement is most likely to be abandoned, because it is too painful not to live up to his positive ego ideal. Of course, this will irritate him, and he will be overcome by feelings of self-doubt, self-loathing, and self-reprimanding behavior.

The continual tension-generating dialectic between the narcissist's grandiosity and his longing for perfection appears to be shame. When a

narcissist feels shame, he feels inadequate, imperfect, and inferior. He has narcissistically harmed himself, and he is now likely to explode in wrath because he feels prominent, exposed, and vulnerable to shame.

9. Boredom

Narcissists have an insatiable want for excitement in order to feel good about themselves, and they are constantly on the lookout for new experiences. Because they are so aggressive, any stimulation allows them to release the rage that is always stored up inside of them. Of course, their anger can take various forms, and boredom is one of their favorites.

When confronted with boredom, the narcissist descends into the abyss of despair, where he revisits old feelings of helplessness and inadequacy derived from previous experiences (for example, feelings of inferiority resulting from an inability to understand lessons in school, or from being bullied, etc.). Boredom causes them concern; it simply destroys their morale, therefore they won't endure it for long. It is precisely these anxious sentiments that drive the individual to seek "narcissistic supply" in the first place. He seeks fame in order to aid him in his never-ending quest.

10. celebrity

One of the reasons the narcissist has an insatiable desire for celebrity is that it leads him to an endless supply of praise and adulation, which he craves in order to fill the "Gap" of his embarrassing upbringing. The narcissist's inability to tolerate shame as a youngster leads to pervasive sentiments of self-disgust and worthlessness.

Because the painful repercussions of shame cannot be controlled, the narcissist devises an efficient strategy to avoid them. He "splits off" from the part of himself that feels guilt on a regular basis, allowing him to "bypass" his shameful feelings. To the untrained eye, bypassed shame appears to be shamelessness or a lack of conscience. The "shamelessness" works by directing the narcissist's shame outward, away from the Self, where nothing is ever his fault, so shielding the narcissist against emotions of self-contempt and unworthiness.

His tried and true method of reducing the impact of such feelings is to get adoration from his never-ending source of narcissistic supply, which he maintains by adopting an attitude of grandiosity and entitlement, which makes him feel famous and unique.

Fame gives him a sense of aliveness, and the more alive he feels, the more he plays to his audience.

His audience reflects back to him his celebrity image and status, and his entire existence is validated. This self-affirmation is manifested in his narcissistic hubris and over-confidence. Hubris relates to the narcissist's extreme self-confidence or pride, and it frequently operates with the notion that punishment will follow if you dare to offend him.

To summarize,
narcissism is a pathological state in which the individual has significant difficulty in his relationships as a direct result of childhood deprivation. The narcissistic behaviors are the narcissist's self-preservative attempts to shield himself from future painful

narcissistic insults as a youngster, through his hostile surroundings and dysfunctional school and family system, his internal regulating system, to put it mildly.

Because the narcissist lacks the internal structures required to counteract
their dreadful feeling of fragmentation, anxiety, and diminishing self-esteem. they resort to these outward behaviors to self-soothe.

As you can see, narcissistic behavior spirals out of control in every setting, resulting in an endless stream of narcissistic victim abuse.

Chapter 3

A narrator's characteristic

Conversational Monopoly

Disobeying Rules or Social Customs

Obsession with Appearance

Unrealistic Expectations

Lack of Concern for Others

More praise, more praise, more praise

It's the fault of everyone else.

They are concerned about abandonment.

The Narcissist Is Immersed in a Fantasy

There are always conditions attached.

Despite its origins in an ancient Greek mythological figure, the modern term "narcissist" usually refers to those who exhibit symptoms of narcissistic personality disorder (NPD). The scientific community recognizes NPD as a psychological disorder and a life-limiting illness. There are numerous theories on the causes and remedies.

Narcissistic traits can have a significant detrimental impact on the mental health of friends, family members, and coworkers.

How Can You Tell If Someone Is a Narcissist?

Movies like "Mommie Dearest," "American Psycho," and "The Wolf of Wall Street" show narcissistic tendencies in society. Narcissists make for interesting theatergoers, but the signs of pathological narcissism aren't usually as obvious in real life.

Several ideas exist among psychologists as to how and why NPD develops in some persons. The underlying assumption of these ideas is that the narcissist suffers a significant psychological wound early in life. This wound is frequently the result of some kind of trauma, such as abuse or neglect. As a result, people suffering from NPD developed a false self.

What are the characteristics of a narcissist?

How to Determine If Someone Is Narcissistic, What are the symptoms of narcissism? Many of the classic narcissistic symptoms stem from their urge to protect itself at all costs. Significant impairments in self and interpersonal functioning are among the American Psychiatric Association Diagnostic and Statistical Manual (DSM-5) criteria for NPD.

The narcissist may exhibit pathological personality traits such as:

•Grandiosity

•Seeking Attention

•Relationships in Disarray

•Empathy Deficiency

•Feelings of Entitlement

NPD is a terminal illness that might be difficult to treat. Narcissists are unlikely to seek treatment on their own. NPD is typically treated with talk therapy. If the individual has other mental health issues or personality problems, mood stabilizers may be utilized.

So, how can you determine if someone is narcissistic? While there are several characteristics that lead to NPD, the following ten are among the most prominent indicators that someone is a narcissistic person.

1. Conversational Monopoly

You may be wondering how to determine if you are a narcissist. One of the most noticeable narcissistic characteristics is monopolizing a conversation. Narcissists speak over or interrupt others during conversations in order to express their opinions or talk about themselves. This behavior can verge on compulsion, intimidating people into complete silence for minutes at a time. They also tend to ignore what others say or respond only superficially before returning the conversation to their story.

These narcissistic characteristics are influenced in part by a/an:

•an overwhelming desire for praise

•a feeling of entitlement

•inability to empathize

Narcissists are oblivious to the need for others to feel seen and heard. The narcissist desires to be the focus of attention.

2. Disobeying Rules or Social Customs

Still want to know how to identify if you're a narcissist?   A propensity to break conventions or traditions, sometimes with spectacular results, is one of the more disruptive symptoms of narcissism. A person with NPD may demand special treatment or feel mistreated if they are unable to work around the system. According to Psychology Today, examples of these narcissistic traits include:

Violation of traffic regulations

stealing office supplies

getting ahead of people in lines

In other words, the rules exist for the benefit of others, not the narcissist. The narcissist is unique. Because of his or her exceptional status, he or she is exempt from the regulations.

3. Obsession with Appearance

The narcissist may be preoccupied with their physical appearance. Every day, some narcissists spend hours in front of a mirror. They are continually fixing or adjusting their appearance. Narcissists are also more likely to discuss other people's appearances. They may degrade someone directly by criticizing:

clothes

body shape

facial characteristics

In addition to their physical appearance, people with NPD are concerned with making a good impression on others. They will exaggerate or manufacture stories to boost their self-esteem and self-importance.

Some persons with NPD expect their family members to be attractive (but not as attractive as the narcissist - think of the evil queen in Snow White). The narcissistic parent may abuse or bully their child, validating their actions because they believe a child is an extension of the parent. A parent suffering from NPD may believe that their children exist solely to make their parents appear good and boost their sense of self-importance. They are useless outside of this context. They don't have their own wants and needs.

However, appearances extend beyond physical appearance. It is also crucial to a narcissist that their lives appear ideal. They are worthy of admiration. The narcissist prioritizes keeping up with the Joneses. Even better if the narcissist can outdo the Joneses.

4. Envy is highlighted.

Another form of narcissistic behavior is jealousy. While most people have sentiments of envy for others at some point in their lives, narcissists might become entirely absorbed by these feelings. They may continuously disparage other people's possessions or good fortune. They may have a strong conviction that others are envious of them.

Some narcissists use this impulse to approach affluent or powerful people and deliberately want to associate with them. In the workplace, sentiments of jealousy motivate the narcissist to steal or minimize the labor of their coworkers. The narcissist may have contributed little to a project. Still, the narcissist may believe he or she is entitled and expects to be at the top of a project.

Narcissists may also believe that someone doing better than them owes them a break at work. The narcissist is envious of others' skills gained through years of hard labor. If the narcissist is unable to acquire those skills, they will make use of a skilled individual. If the narcissist is unable to manipulate
someone to acquire what they want, they may attempt to drive their coworker out of the company.

This deceitful behavior reduces the narcissist's competition, at least temporarily.

5. Lack of Concern for Others

Narcissists frequently engage in manipulative behavior and utilize their interactions with others to advance their own aims. People with NPD form significant emotional bonds with friends or family members, and they use the connection to benefit themselves and increase their self-esteem.

This form of manipulation can include the following:

•extreme mood swings

•heated debates

•a desire to place blame on others

In severe cases, a narcissist may become enraged at others if they perceive a slight change. If someone in the narcissist's family becomes ill, for example, the narcissist may be negligent at best and nasty at worst. They have difficulty acknowledging the suffering of others because they lack empathy.

6. More praise, more praise, more praise
Narcissists are the group's movie stars. They have an excessive sense of self-importance and expect to be adored wherever they go.

Narcissists also want frequent praise and special attention from others, even when it is undeserved. Narcissists assure their narcissistic supply by situating and monopolizing the topic.

So be it if others feel cheated in the process. The narcissist gets what he or she wants at the expense of others. This includes compliments.

Furthermore, as Healthline.com points out, the narcissist puts himself or herself in the way of compliments if they do not come readily. The narcissist seeks praises on their beauty, cooking, work, or life, a behavior known as fishing. Anything to demonstrate their significance.

Although they appear confident on the surface, they are consumed by self-doubt, which challenges their feeling of self-importance. If they do not receive praise at regular intervals, they begin to feel cheated. This motivates people to seek out more compliments.

The narcissist requires someone who continuously elevates them. Their superficial charm quickly makes them a crowd favorite. Compliments come

easy for them. However, the infatuation phase is short-lived. The narcissist's desire for praise and excessive attention could not be satisfied by a bottomless pit.

Unfortunately, if they do not receive the amount of praise they expect, the narcissist explodes. This wrath is frequently the initial step in the cycle of abuse for narcissists who turn physically abusive.

If they can, people with NPD gain admiration and appreciation through charm. The slightest criticism or damage to their self-image may be enough to push them over the edge. If they do not receive recognition, they will resort to other, often highly damaging and even hazardous, methods to obtain what they believe they deserve.

If the contrary occurs, that is, the narcissist receives criticism, the situation frequently becomes combustible. Again, the narcissist may demonstrate angry symptoms verging on wrath.

Unfortunately, the person who was the target of the fury may not have criticized the narcissist at all. Instead, the narcissist saw the person's words or action as a slight and responded accordingly. Everything stems from the narcissist's low self-esteem. Given the degree of arrogance displayed by many narcissists, it's difficult for their victims to accept that the narcissists' poor self-esteem is crippling them. Yes, it does.

Many narcissists will go to considerable measures to boost their own ego and gain the necessary plaudits. This is one of the most visible symptoms of

narcissism. According to Psychology Today, some narcissists crave praise and admiration so much that they choose high-profile positions in business or politics to satisfy this need.

This obsessive desire for adoration is the result of a wounded and shattered inner child. Because of this wound, the youngster created a fake self in order to be accepted and safe in a hazardous situation. To the narcissist, an attack on his or her fake self seems like annihilation. The narcissist combats these feelings of inferiority by receiving comments and admiration from others.

7. It's the fault of everyone else.

According to Very Well Mind, shaming and blaming are two crucial techniques in the narcissist's manipulation toolbox. The narcissist wields power over these toxic twins. The narcissist elevates themselves in their relationships by demeaning their spouse. The victim is always at a disadvantage. If the victim upsets the balance of power, the narcissist will do whatever it takes to recover control.

This power is obtained by the narcissist by:

being impolite,

by putting someone down,

by concealing themselves behind nasty jokes,
by critiquing

as well as by sabotage.

For example, if a person is uncomfortable about his or her weight, he or she may become the brunt of the narcissist's fat jokes, or they may avoid the joke entirely and be quite frank. Because they lack empathy, narcissists frequently disguise their statements as well-meaning. "I'm just concerned for your health," a narcissist could claim after insulting someone over their weight at a public lunch.

When the victim objects, the narcissist shames him or her into silence, reminding the victim that the remark was made for the victim's own good. To make a point, the narcissist may say that the victim is overly sensitive. This prevents the victim from defending himself or herself against the narcissist's assault.

Unfortunately, this exposes the person to additional mental health abuse. This type of public shaming raises the potential that others within hearing distance will follow suit. When this occurs, the victim is subjected to more than simply the narcissist's shaming methods. He or she is subjected to the group's humiliation strategy.

There is also a propensity in more subtle narcissists to blame everyone else for their actions and failings. If a child receives a "B" on his or her report card, they are held responsible for making the parent look terrible. A victim of domestic violence is blamed for causing the narcissist to hurt him or her. If the narcissist has a neglected spouse, the child may be blamed for diverting the spouse's attention away from the narcissist.

It is never the narcissist's fault in these instances. By blaming others, the narcissist absolves themselves of responsibility for their lives and actions. The narcissist is rarely aware of their role in a poor circumstance. They believe that those who do not follow their internal, well-choreographed script intend to hurt them.

The majority of people are unaware of the narcissist's internal script. Unfortunately, they don't find out until the narcissist explodes when someone deviates from the script. A narcissist with this attitude is always looking for someone to blame and abuse.

It also places the narcissist in a position of power. People close to the narcissist must walk on eggshells in order to maintain their emotional well-being. They never know when the narcissist may invent an incident to accuse them for, which keeps the narcissist's victims on their toes.

8. They are concerned about abandonment.

Most narcissists, according to mental health professionals, display these maladaptive behaviors as a result of their fear of abandonment. However, as strange as it may sound, it is usually the narcissist that abandons people. It's often a matter of leaving before you're left in the mind of a narcissist.

However, despite being instigated by the narcissist, these breakups rarely last. Victims of this breakup, then makeup cycle must recognize that this cycle is caused by a number of causes.

To begin, the narcissist requires his or her narcissistic supply in order to feel good. Coming back to someone the narcissist has rejected makes perfect sense to him or her. The narcissist has already groomed that person to offer them the adulation that the narcissist requires.

Second, the process of leaving and returning repeatedly wears the victim down. After a while, the victim's self-esteem suffers greatly. The victim becomes dependent on the narcissist while the pattern of leaving and returning continues. This guarantees that the victim will never abandon the narcissist.

The narcissist engages in "love bombing," or coming on really strong to their target at first, establishing dependency. This is the stuff of lousy romance novels, and it's one of the most obvious indications of narcissism. Nobody loves the victim as much as the narcissist does. Indeed, narcissists pay such close attention to their victims that the victims believe no one will ever love them as much as their narcissist does.

Because love bombing produces such a high, the victim develops a craving for it. However, for the narcissist, this is simply the beginning of the valuing, then depreciating process. At first, the narcissist elevates others. The narcissist's attention object can do no wrong.
However, things swiftly turn nasty. The narcissist's dread of abandonment persists. They gradually depreciate his or her object

of affection. By doing so, the narcissist lessens the impact of the abandonment they fear is just

around the corner. Again, the narcissist may cut ties with the victim in order to prevent being abandoned. The victim, on the other hand, has the option of flipping the situation by breaking up with the narcissist. This behavior sends the narcissist into overdrive. More love bombing occurs in order to keep the victim in the narcissist's grip.

In the most severe circumstances, the narcissist lashes out at the victim for ending their relationship. The narcissist may then launch a campaign to harm the victim's reputation or attempt to steal the victim's friends. In the worst-case scenario, physical assault may occur when the victim abandons the narcissist. The narcissist will not let anyone leave. Physical violence or the threat of physical violence frequently puts an end to the abandonment, at least temporarily.

9. The Narcissist Is Immersed in a Fantasy

A narcissist frequently has grandiose fantasies. They concoct complex fantasies about their extraordinary life and fortune. They expect others to share and reinforce their fantasies. The narcissist's delusions are diverse and may include the following:

Everyone else's more lovely and talented,

Smarter and wealthier

What is more important

Covert narcissists will fabricate stories about events that never occurred to support their fantasies. If the event did occur, they will alter the facts to make it appear larger, better, and brighter than it was. They mix with governors, millionaires, and movie stars in the narcissist's world. Adoring fans prostrate themselves at their feet. When and if someone challenges their irrational sense of superiority, the narcissist goes on a rant. This stems from their desire to safeguard the false self that they built so long ago.

While their actions have an impact on everyone around them, the true mental health harm began a long time ago with some form of trauma. To survive their trauma, they were forced to build a new, more acceptable self. To support this weak, fake ego, they developed a fantasy life.
If the narcissist's dream loses support, their phony self crumbles. This isn't an explanation for the narcissist's frequently

terrible behavior or overblown feeling of self-importance. It does, however, explain why the narcissist's fantasy is so significant.

10. There are always conditions attached.

Victims who are aware of the narcissist's methods understand that gifts come with strings attached. Unsolicited presents are used by the narcissist to persuade the victim into giving them what they desire. They never give a present just for the sake of giving a gift.

Gifts, whether real or intangible, are given in exchange for something else. The narcissist always makes certain that the recipient understands who

donated the gift. There is an implicit understanding with the narcissist as well. The narcissist will get their collateral later.

It's much better if the person getting it is in a bad mood. The narcissist is capable of rescuing this victim from severe conditions. In exchange, the receiver pays again and again. The narcissist offers to instill loyalty, ensuring that no one ever abandons them. Sometimes the narcissist provides so much that some others become dependent on them.

Unfortunately for the victim of this narcissistic strategy, accepting gifts from anyone is difficult. The victim is always afraid that the gifts will come with strings attached, which has an impact on their mental health. Victims of narcissists have a tough time believing the intentions of others, even when those intentions are excellent.

Finally, how can you tell whether someone is a narcissist?
While NPD is a recognized psychological condition, there are many unknowns and

uncertainties. NPD patients present numerous diagnostic and clinical problems. Unfortunately, people with NPD are frequently protective about their personality. They may be resistant to intervention. They do not seek help from a licensed therapist or any mental health expert. Nonetheless, understanding the symptoms of NPD (and other personality disorders) is the first step toward correcting manipulative conduct. Victims of narcissistic behavior must take actions to alleviate the harm caused by the narcissist.

Establish Limits

First, victims must establish boundaries. Narcissists by nature exploit people because they lack empathy for the plight of others. They endeavor to meet their demands, frequently by dubious ways. To survive, individuals around them must establish firm and unambiguous boundaries and be willing to enforce them.

Everyone is entitled to healthy relationships. If you have been a victim of domestic violence or abuse, the National Domestic Violence Hotline can help. Simply dial 1-800-799-SAFE or visit www.TheHotline.org.

Recognize Your Value

Second, the victims of the narcissist should understand that what the narcissist does never reflects the victims' worthiness. While the narcissist may dish out abuse that appears to be very personal, it isn't. It stems from the narcissist's profound sense of inadequacy. This is not to mean that the victim of the narcissist should not defend himself or herself. This activity, however, should come from a place of self-care.

Take a step back.

Finally, self-care may imply distance from the narcissist. It is sometimes sufficient to limit a person's exposure to the narcissist. However, it is possible that the victim will no longer see the narcissist. Walking away gets a little simpler for someone who understands narcissism's features. The individual who fully understands what the narcissist is about recognizes the warning flags for what they are.

Chapter 4:

The Narcissistic abuser's weapon

If you're the victim, your emotions are the most powerful weapon a narcissist has against you. They use this against you as a weapon. They accomplish this through the initial "LOVE BOMB PHASE" - telling you how amazing you are! Basically, you believe you are perfect and cannot make a mistake. It's almost as if you're "God-like".

This is the stage in the "Get to Know You" process where you let down your guard and begin to share your experiences about previous relationships, work experiences, and family life "The Good, Bad, and Ugly" with them.

This is a typical element of starting a new relationship or friendship with someone because it helps us create trust and rapport with them and assess whether we have similar beliefs/values and interests in life. Whether we continue to get to know one another at this point or say "Nice to meet you, see ya!"

However, for the Narcissist, this is a critical stage in determining whether it is worthwhile for them to invest their valuable time on YOU. They are tuned in to every word you say, every emotion you show, and every outcome (including achievements and failures) in your life.

They make mental notes on how to use all of this information (words, ideas, emotions, and actions) against you as a Weapon of Mass Destruction in the future to intimidate and manipulate you into submission.

Chameleons are narcissists. They will change their behavior, vocabulary, and often agree with all you say about your thoughts, beliefs, and life hurts to fit the potential victim.

It will feel as if you have been seen, heard, and recognized as a human being for the first time.

What happens when they realize they have you? BOOM! With the Narcissist, this is where the fun and games begin. If you work in sales or business, you'll recognize the following analogy.

During the "Love Bomb" stage, the Narcissist qualifies as their next target. The Narcissist has a "Target Market," or "Avatar." They decide if this individual is a "Right Fit" or "Fit for Purpose" for them or whether they should "walk away" since they will quickly realize that this person will be too difficult to influence.

They will be drawn to you if you are an Empath or have previously been a "Victim" of Narcissistic Abuse or have had prior "Abuse" of any kind that has lowered your self worth/ self image. They can detect you.

You'll gravitate toward them because you adore the way they make you feel. Subconsciously, it develops into an addiction. As if it were a drug. This is where I assist clients in rebuilding their self-worth and self-confidence if they have taken a hammering at work as a result of a Narcissist. A Narcissist might be "Hot and Cold" in your presence.
They idolize you and want to speak your praises to the world one minute because you've accomplished something and it makes them seem good to show you off the next. Then they abandon you by undervaluing your self-worth, especially if

they notice your self-worth rising and they believe they are losing power over you.

You will become aware of the hot and cold effect, and you will begin to question, "What have I done wrong?" We were so fantastic at first, and now I can't rekindle that relationship/feeling." So you start working harder to prove your worth to them and regain that "Feeling." Sometimes the Narcissist will accept what you've done, but not as openly as in the past. So you continue to work harder and HARDER! Until you exhaust yourself!

The Narcissist will drain you. They are the most blatant impostors around.

Have you ever had a supervisor that appeared to be too wonderful to be true? They spoke all the right things, but their actions were off? The "Smoke and Mirrors Effect" is what I call this. However, these are the bosses who are promoted because they know HOW to manage up! Especially if their supervisors are based in another country, as most are these days if you work for a multinational corporation.

I've gotten fairly skilled at spotting Narcissists, so it doesn't take long for me to spot them. I believe they are aware that I am aware, and I have had several situations where this has occurred.

The phrase "Character Assassination" comes to mind.
It used to bother me because I pride myself on my work ethic and honesty, but now that I'm a Limited Edition Leader - embracing my actual authentic self - I don't mind. I don't mind since I know who I am and how I function. This is demonstrated by what I say and do.

My deeds are mirrored in my words. I care about the people with whom I work. I build long-term connections, not one-sided "what can you do for me today" transactions. I don't care where you are in the work hierarchy. If your beliefs do not line with mine, then you are not someone I would waste my time with.

What matters is that my Professional Brand precedes me.

Finally, I want people to recall my working connection with them as

"Yes I know Paula, I loved working with her.....because of how she made me feel..."

When providing a service, results are expected, but how you make someone feel while working with you and beyond is priceless! That beats "Status and Title" every time.

When you are given the opportunity to make a difference in the world, your status and title are an honor. Use it to serve others rather than yourself.

The goal of Limited Edition Leadership is to strengthen your internal foundations.
So, when the external environment comes into play, you aren't simply tossed around like a leaf in the wind. Too often, persons in positions of leadership are readily swayed by external influences, since as you advance in the ranks, you will face more of these types of people or "strong willed emotionally volatile individuals" who will often feel threatened by what you're sending out.

If you are a Limited Edition Leader, they will activate you. Because you have the "X"

Factor that they lack. YOU ARE THE X-FACTOR!

They will bring you down in order to elevate themselves inside an organization. The classic Survival of the Fittest scenario. Since the GFC in 2008, I've seen this play out even more in my Pharmaceutical Industry.
As a result, being a Limited Edition Leader is more important than ever to distinguish.

To summarize, your most powerful weapon against these individuals is your internal "Thoughts and Emotions," which govern your professional decisions and behaviors. Master those two things, and you'll have mastered not only yourself, but also those around you, including those pesky Narcs.

Chapter 5

how to deactivate your abuser

How to Disarm a Narcissist

How to Resist Narcissistic Abuse

Dealing with a narcissist can be a very difficult experience. Their capacity to keep one step ahead of others and their propensity to steamroll others might leave you feeling powerless.

But don't worry; there are practical ways for disarming a narcissist and regaining control of the situation.

How does a Narcissist try to gain an advantage?

To properly outwit a narcissist, you must first understand how they operate.

Narcissists are masters of psychological manipulation and gaslighting, adopting a wide range of techniques to exercise control and make you doubt your sanity.
Understanding the intricacies of a narcissist's mind allows you to recognize their ploys and protect your own well-being.

The following are some of the tools that a narcissist will employ to try to bend you to their will:

How to Deal with Narcissistic Abuse

Manipulation of Perception: Gaslighting

Gaslighting is a narcissistic manipulation technique used to make you doubt your own version of events.
They will purposefully mislead and twist the truth, producing a warped world that will

make you doubt your memory and perception.

They gain power and control over you by spreading seeds of doubt in your mind.

Gaslighting strategies used by narcissists include:

Denial and Contradiction: They will deny saying or doing something despite proof to the contrary. They may even contradict themselves, making it difficult to believe your own memory of events.

Selective Amnesia: Narcissists "forget" essential data or conversations in order to distort your perception of a situation. This selective memory helps to devalue your experiences while imposing their version of reality on you.

When confronted with the consequences of their conduct, narcissists frequently shift blame to others. They will accuse you of misinterpreting their words or behavior, which will cause you to doubt your own judgment.

Mind Games: Experimenting with Your Emotions

Narcissists are skilled at using mind games to confuse and dominate their victims.

They use a variety of techniques to keep you off balance and manipulate your emotions.

Some examples of common mind games are

Words and actions that contradict each other: Narcissists may say one thing and do the opposite, leaving you perplexed and unaware of their genuine intentions.

This paradoxical behavior is a purposeful strategy to keep you anxious and on edge. Manipulators frequently employ guilt and shame as methods to induce obedience. They will try to shame you into submitting to their wishes by making you feel bad for asserting your boundaries.

Emotional Withdrawal: As a form of control, narcissists remove affection, attention, or support on a regular basis. They instill fear of abandonment or rejection in you, making you more vulnerable to their demands.

Dominating the Conversation via Control: Narcissists thrive on establishing their authority and directing conversations in order to further their own agenda.

To keep control, they deploy a variety of strategies, including

Interrupting and Speaking Over Others: Narcissists constantly interrupt and speak over others, ignoring their thoughts and opinions. This strategy allows them to keep control of the debate and stifle competing viewpoints.
They may drown out your voice by monopolizing the conversation, leaving little room for your participation. They weaken your sense of worth and cement their authority by dominating your voice.

Topic Redirecting and Manipulation: Narcissists are masters at redirecting talks to their advantage. They will steer talks away from themes that would test their ego or expose their manipulative behavior, allowing them to keep control of the narrative.

Manipulating the Truth with Lies, Lies, and More Lies: Narcissists are adept liars who will go to any length to maintain their superiority complex.
They strategically utilize lies to get an advantage and manipulate people around them. Common strategies include:

False Promises: Narcissists frequently make extravagant promises that they do not intend to keep. This technique is known as future faking. They utilize these promises to influence and control others, luring them deeper into their web.

False charges: When forced to make false charges against others, narcissists will resort to them. These unfounded charges attempt to discredit and alienate their targets, ensuring that the narcissist is supported by others.

Fabricated Facts: Narcissists distort reality by fabricating stories and changing facts. They will alter events to fit their story, leaving you befuddled and questioning your own understanding of reality.

Let's look at some tactics for disarming a narcissist now that we've looked at some of the ways they will try to dominate and manipulate you.

What Is the Best Way to Disarm a Narcissist?

The greatest method to disarm a narcissist is to anticipate their tactics and believe in your own strength.

Here are some pointers on how to go about it.

•Maintain Your Calm
When dealing with a narcissist, staying calm is a vital weapon.
It allows you to keep control of your emotions and prevents them from taking advantage of your reactions.

You may negotiate challenging interactions with greater resilience and protect your personal well-being by using these tactics.

•Recognize Your Triggers
Recognize what causes your emotional reaction when interacting with a narcissist. You can better prepare yourself and build coping techniques to remain calm by identifying these triggers.

•Emotional Regulation

Learn skills for controlling your emotions, such as deep breathing exercises, mindfulness, or visualization. These activities can help you stay balanced and grounded in the face of adversity.

•Take Your Time to Respond

Instead of reacting rashly, take a minute to pause and gather your thoughts before responding. This helps you to answer thoughtfully rather
than engaging in a heated debate that the narcissist may take advantage of.

•Maintain Your Focus on Facts

Narcissists frequently twist the truth or deceive their victims. Focus on objective truths and retain a clear awareness of reality to counteract this. Avoid becoming entangled in their web of deception.

Keep a record of your interactions with the narcissist, including dates, times, and specifics of talks or situations. This record can be used as evidence and to keep your cool in the face of gaslighting or manipulation.

Make Use of These Assertive Phrases

When dealing with a narcissist who is attempting to influence you, adopting the proper phrases will assist defuse the situation and allow you the time you need to devise an outwitting strategy.

Here are some statements that therapists and professionals recommend using while attempting to disarm a narcissist in such a situation.

"I understand your perspective, but…"

"Let's focus on finding a solution that works for both of us."

"I appreciate your input, but I need some time to think about it."

"Can we approach this discussion with dignity?""
I cherish our relationship and wish to establish a healthy manner of communicating with each other.

"Let's try to find common ground and move forward together."

"I'm open to hearing your thoughts, but let's keep the conversation respectful."

"I'm feeling overwhelmed right now; can we discuss this later?""

"I hear what you're saying, but I have a different perspective."

"It's important to me that we address this issue in a calm and constructive manner."

Why are these sentences useful in disarming a narcissist?

These sentences are useful at disarming a narcissist because they promote good communication, establish limits, and shift the power dynamics in the relationship.

Recognizing their point of view
By acknowledging their point of view, you demonstrate that you are prepared to listen and consider their viewpoint. This can assist

to calm them down and make them more amenable to a constructive conversation.

Looking for a win-win situation

Narcissists frequently desire to maintain control and have their way with things. By proposing a solution that benefits all parties, you introduce the concept of compromise and teamwork, which can disarm their need for domination.

Taking time to reflect

By requesting time to contemplate or analyze information, you can create space and avoid impulsive reactions. This can keep the narcissist from playing with your emotions in the heat of the moment.

Maintaining a healthy relationship by emphasizing respect

Power battles and demeaning people are what narcissists thrive on. You steer the discourse toward more productive and courteous interactions by highlighting the value of respect and the desire for a healthy partnership.

expressing many points of view

While acknowledging another point of view is crucial, stating your own demonstrates that you have boundaries and individual opinions. This can put them on the defensive and provide room for a more balanced discourse.

Later revisiting the conversation

When you're feeling overwhelmed, asking to return to the topic later allows you to restore your composure and tackle the discussion more calmly. It

prevents the narcissist from taking advantage of your emotional fragility at that time.

Overall, these statements are intended to establish limits, retain respect, and promote a more collaborative and productive attitude to communication.

They can disarm a narcissist by confronting their deceptive tactics and establishing a more balanced dynamic in the discussion.

Maintain Clear Boundaries

If the preceding sentences do not work, it is evident that the narcissist has no intention of giving you space. It is critical in such instances that you communicate and maintain your boundaries.

In a calm and authoritative manner, convey your boundaries to the narcissist. Make use of "I" expressions to describe how their actions affect you and what you will not tolerate.

Once you've established your boundaries, stick to them. Narcissists may push your buttons, but it's critical to be solid and unwavering in your expectations.

"I will not tolerate insults or belittlement directed at me." I'm leaving if you don't tone down your profanity."

"If you shout, I will leave the room."

"I will not discuss this with you if you are going to be disrespectful."

"I don't deserve to be treated like this, and I won't tolerate it."

"If you continue talking to me with that tone, I will put the phone down."

Obviously, after you've established the limit, you must keep to it and follow through on the consequences. This will give a clear message to the narcissist that they will be unable to control or manipulate you.

Take a step back.
In some cases, it may be necessary to take the decisive step of leaving the situation totally.

This is especially important when dealing with a narcissist who abuses others or continuously disregards logic and empathy. Recognizing your own limitations and being willing to leave a harmful atmosphere is an act of self-preservation.

It could be the end of a relationship, leaving a job, or even leaving a social event. You are prioritizing your mental and emotional well-being by doing so, refusing to expose yourself to continued mistreatment.

Walking away sends the narcissist a strong message that their behavior is inappropriate and will not be allowed.

You adopt a hard stand against their manipulation and control by demonstrating your determination to protect yourself.

It emphasizes your independence and affirms your refusal to be caught in a destructive dynamic.

They should be ignored.
One successful method for coping with a narcissist is to simply ignore them.

Because narcissists thrive on attention and approval, denying them what they desire takes away their power.

You keep control of your emotions and behaviors by refusing to acknowledge their attempts to agitate or manipulate you.

This can be achieved by not responding to their provocations, disengaging from talks, or even physically removing yourself from their presence.

Keep in mind that your silence can be a powerful statement in and of itself.

Do not get drawn into their games.

Narcissists are experts in the dark art of mind games.

It's critical to understand that these games are intended to perplex and undermine you. Falling for their ruses just serves to maintain their control cycle.

Keep an eye out for their tactics, which may involve gaslighting, projection, guilt-tripping, or subtle types of manipulation. Allow yourself to become entangled in their web of deception.

Instead, concentrate on remaining rooted in your own truth and reality.

Trust your intuition and seek the advice of reliable friends or family members who can offer an objective viewpoint.

Do Not Retaliate

Another good tactic for dealing with a narcissist is to avoid direct confrontation, as this can play into their hands.

When you fight back, you risk giving the narcissist fodder to misinterpret your words and actions, allowing them to depict themselves as the victim while painting you negatively. They will essentially use your reaction against you.

Instead of fighting a war you are unlikely to win, consider walking away from the situation entirely.

You deny the narcissist the gratification of eliciting an emotional response or dragging you into their web of deception by disengaging.

Not fighting back does not suggest weakness or surrender.

On the contrary, it shows courage and self-preservation. It enables you to safeguard your mental well-being and avoid becoming further involved in their destructive dynamics.

Maintain your center and focus on your truth.

Maintaining a clear perspective in the midst of a narcissist's maelstrom of manipulation can be difficult.

To get an advantage, they will manipulate facts, change history, and even outright lies.

However, it is critical to be centered and grounded in your own reality.

By remaining grounded, you create inner steadiness and clarity.

This gives you the ability to see through their web of falsehoods and deception.

Trust your intuition and stand firm in your views and principles, refusing to be misled by their attempts to undermine your self-assurance.

Make Use of Your Support Network

Another excellent method for disarming a narcissist is to rely on your support system.

The narcissist will do everything they can to isolate you, but remember that you have friends and family who care about you and want to assist.

When the narcissist's manipulations distort your vision, these people can provide crucial insights, emotional support, and serve as a reality check.
Reach out to people you trust and tell them about your experiences.

By talking about your contacts with narcissists, you allow others to perceive the problem from a different angle and help you obtain clarity.
They can throw insight on the narcissist's behavior patterns, validate your feelings, and offer advice on how to deal with challenging situations.
Your support network can also assist you in maintaining your self-esteem and confidence, which are frequently eroded by the techniques of a narcissist.
They will remind you of your intrinsic worth, reaffirm your limits, and give you the

confidence to stand up for yourself when necessary.

Consider obtaining professional assistance from therapists or support organizations that specialize in psychological abuse.

These websites provide specialist insights and coping skills to assist you in navigating the intricacies of living with a narcissist.

Last Words on How to Disarm a Narcissist

Dealing with a narcissist can be excruciating. However, by putting the tactics mentioned in this essay into action, you may effectively disarm them and defend your own safety.

Never forget that a narcissist cannot be changed. So concentrate on your own personal growth, healing, and development.

Invest your energy on things that will bring you closer to your goals and happiness.

Chapter 6

An abuser's psychological profile

A significant amount of effort has gone into developing a psychological profile of an abuser. However, research has yet to yield reliable empirical data. Having said that, there is evidence that certain characteristics are shared by all abusers.

Boys and girls have always been taught various things as they grow up. Girls are taught to be cautious and sensitive by society. They learn how to be lovely and make their dolls pretty, as well as how to be polite and caring.

Boys, on the other hand, are more likely to receive toys that promote bravery and fearlessness. And they are frequently placed in contact sports. The idea is for them to become strong, tough guys capable of protecting all of the girls. But they can't reveal even the slightest sign of weakness.

Social impact and traditional values are determining variables.

The media has a significant impact on gender disparities in children. The same characters appear in movies and television shows: the buff cop, the male guardian of the family, and the macho superhero. And, while they've just begun to gingerly introduce female versions, relatively few films feature a woman saving a man.

In general, an abuser is someone who has highly conservative views and was raised in a sexist atmosphere. They internalize all of these things as children and grow up to be adults who see themselves accordingly.

An abuser's psychological profile

Given the factors given, you may fairly infer that the victims are mostly women, while the abusers are mostly men. Such assumptions are supported by statistics. And now we'll show you some of their most distinguishing characteristics.

Biases in cognition: strict psychology

Abusers frequently have erroneous perceptions of gender roles. They consider the other gender as inferior to them, which justifies their brutality. They are filled with preconceptions that cause them to respond violently.

Because of their intolerance, they are authoritarian, inflexible, and anti-democratic. Their rigidity of thought causes them to take things personally. They provide no room for other points of view.

A failure to solve problems

Their lack of mental flexibility will prevent them from finding solutions to their difficulties. This could be because they have a polar, or dichotomous, cognitive pattern. That is, people place themselves on one of two extremes, excellent or bad. There is no room for compromise or moderation.

Evidence suggests that they perceive things in black and white because that is how they were raised. They are frequently the children of severe and militaristic parents.

Self-esteem issues

Their upbringing shaped their emotional development. As a result, an abuser's psychological profile is concentrated on low self-esteem. This loss of self-esteem could be the cause or result of abuse. This, of course, is never justified.

The issue is that they are unaware of their lack of self-esteem. Instead of working on their self-esteem, they opt to be passive-aggressive in almost every aspect of their lives.

Communication difficulties

This passive hostile demeanor reveals their inability to communicate effectively with others. In fact, lack of assertiveness is one of the most distinguishing characteristics of an abuser's psychological profile.

They enforce their power and norms by bitterness, obstinacy, or sloth. Abusive persons are rarely forceful, thus they rarely express themselves directly or explicitly.

Dependence on emotions

The main result of this wear and tear in their connections with others is social isolation. Because they lack friendship, they devote their entire attention to their spouse.

Their romantic relationship will gradually deteriorate into an obsession. Because they regard the other person as their only source of intimacy or support, they develop emotional reliance. They continue to demand more, and the relationship becomes quite unhealthy.

Control is required.

Abusers feel compelled and obligated to exert control over everything their partner does or feels. Their jobs, family relationships, social group, interests... They acquire intense watchfulness and unhealthful jealousy.

Frustration

Abusers frequently vent their hatred and resentment at home as a result of workplace frustration. They are easily irritated and have poor impulse control. This type of aggression, known as expressive violence, frequently becomes more intense as more violent occurrences occur.

There is no self-control or empathy.

An abuser's psychological profile includes a lack of emotional control. Abusers lack emotional literacy. They have a difficult time expressing their emotions. They have no idea how to reflect, and they lack empathy. This is what prevents them from feeling guilty about the agony and devastation they've caused their victim.

Lies that are seductive

Abusers usually win over their victims through seduction. They are deceptive individuals who employ lies and false promises. And they can play a variety of roles to obtain what they desire.

Although each instance is unique, these characteristics provide an overall picture of an abuser's psychological profile. In general, they appear to be selfish, sexist, and manipulative individuals. Psychological assault is their primary mode of interaction with others.

A true story of psychological abuse

I had the opportunity to live with people who were much younger than me a few years ago. I might not have met them if I hadn't decided to return to school. They were between my generation and my own children's generation in age.

Something piqued my interest, particularly among the females. They became deeply immersed in abusive relationships without even realizing it. Is that all their future has in store for them?

They would tell me about their "fights" and conflicts with their boyfriends. It sounded the same every time.

To begin, they would explain why they were angry, how they reached a breaking point, and close the story with a sense of guilt or blame. Something along the lines of "I have a really bad temper," "He hasn't done anything really bad..."

To be honest, their stories made me shudder. They were things a girl should never have to put up with. Even if they didn't agree with how they were being handled, these females would make up explanations for all of their terrible behavior. I'm sure if they thought about it objectively, they'd disagree with the arguments they adhered to so fiercely.

Some mornings, I'd see them come in with a melancholy expression on their face. They would tell us about what happened during the break till everything inside spilled out. It was very clear. That was not the expression of a young woman in love.

It was the face of someone in a poisonous and dependent relationship, one rife with psychological abuse.

We didn't know about psychological abuse back then.

I really wanted to feel like myself and give my son a great childhood. The ideal childhood I imagined was conceivable in the concept of the "happy family" I had always desired.

When I became pregnant, his genuine self began to emerge. He began to mistreat me, yelling, insulting, and fighting with me over little matters. He made me feel insignificant and incapable of accomplishing anything. Without him, who was I?

Everything worsened after I had my son.
Things worsened when my son was born. He even assaulted me when I was holding the baby. I tried to avoid arguments as much as possible after that. I rushed away from his rage, allowing myself to be persuaded by a simple "I'm sorry."
They were becoming more common. I became entangled in the web of psychological abuse.
Most of the time, I thought I was to blame. Was it my terrible temper that was to blame? He quit working and began assisting around the house. When he drank a beer, he transformed into the Devil himself. He verbally abused me and hit and broke anything in his reach. But I had one lovely aim in mind: a happy family. I reminded

myself that every partnership has disagreements.

I avoided him when he fought with me. It was unimaginable that I would have to deal with my parents' yelling and insults in my own home. That destructive attitude was the worst part.
It does not heal; instead, it grows deeper by the day.
When our son was three years old, he began abusing him. To humiliate him in the same way he humiliated me.
Our son was an easy target for all of the rage he harbored inside. Hatred. Why? I'll never find out. But I know he always sought to keep a victim close by. We were clearly dissatisfied.

My buddies were critical in bringing me back to reality.

I gradually expanded my social circle. Despite the fact that I was already a recluse, I found new friends. And I saw — or was pushed to see — that these battles weren't typical.

He was destroying my self-esteem.

I toiled away within and outside our home, hoping to bring home some money. In the summer, after nine or ten hours of serving tables, I retreated for a few hours with my pals.

Sweet comments of support and affection brought me some solace. However, when winter arrived, I returned to my jail. The dream of a happy family felt further and further away with each passing day.

My son was three years old, and I hadn't looked at myself in the mirror in two years. I had lost all interest in making myself appear nice. For what purpose? I was unsightly and exhausted.

At the age of thirty, I felt elderly.

At the few gatherings we attended, he would constantly shout and belittle me. Nothing he did was acceptable or correct. My eyes became cloudy with sadness, like the sea on a moonless night.

This served as a warning to me. This was not the intended outcome.

Being conscious of it exacerbated my misery.

I came to believe that this life I had chosen was entirely my responsibility, that it was entirely my fault. And I lied to everyone about our connection.

I made up reasons until I convinced everyone that my hair loss was due to a hormone imbalance.

Something snapped one day, and my body told my mind that enough was enough. I suffered a panic attack that led me directly to the gates of death.
My body gradually stopped working. I initially lost sensation in my fingers, then in my hands and feet. Then there was my face, mouth, arms, and legs... My breathing became irregular as a result.

This is not something I would wish on anyone. To watch your body gradually quit operating. My buddies drove me to the hospital, where I stayed for the night for observation. He marched our child home. Aside from being a buddy, the doctor in that small town was also a psychiatrist. He suggested that I spend the remainder of the week at a friend's house for calm and rehabilitation.

"No" became second nature to me.

That was the start of my recovery, which lasted 5 days till I returned home. He was standing on the porch. I hugged him as I headed up the stairs. "I'm

back, and I'm feeling so much better," I told him. He rejected me with a shove that knocked me off my feet.

He started yelling at me, but I don't recall what he said. I couldn't hear him any more. I could only see how afraid I was by his rants, shoves, and the brutality in his movements and words.

I was terrified for myself, my child, and the friend who had come to the house with me.

"Run!" was the only thought that sprang to mind. But I couldn't go without my 5-year-old son, who I was worried would injure him only to hurt me. That's what I assumed he'd do to retaliate against me. But I hadn't accomplished anything!
We left horrified, the hair on our arms standing on end. Nobody said anything the entire way to my friend's place. We were deafeningly quiet when we arrived. He arrived a few minutes later. I went out onto the second-floor patio and spotted him.

He expressed his regret one more time.
But, guess what? It had already been too late. One word emerged from the depths of my spirit. "NO!! It's too much for me. "I'm finished with you!" I had decided to break free from the cage of psychological torment.

I wanted him to be happy alone because he didn't seem to be with me, and I told him how much I loved him. He's only called with death threats as a result of the split. He has threatened me with retaliation for the humiliation.

We do not want to see him. When he's around, he causes us harm. He drags my son and myself down with him. Being away is the only way I can get what I need: serenity for myself and, most importantly, peace for my son. I will not let anyone, not even his soul, harm him.

It is my responsibility as a mother to teach him not to mix love and humiliation.

...because if someone loves you, they will not psychologically abuse you.

Chapter 7

Reclaim your power and your identity

Many of the things you do so freely: saying 'yes' to things you should say 'no' to; acting in ways that are not congruent with your Truth - just to get love, validation, and approval; staying in toxic places and relationships, etc., are ways in which you give your power away.

I understand how risky that is.

I've done it a million times before. That is why I wanted to share with you a list of things you can do to reclaim your power, reconnect with yourself, and live the life you deserve.

7 Effective Steps to Regaining Your Power and Being True to Yourself

1. Say 'no' when it is necessary and with conviction.

The vast majority of people are unaware of how perilous it is to say 'yes' all of the time. How destructive it is to continually try to please everyone around you at the expense of betraying yourself. And, while we all fall into this trap from time to time, if you begin saying 'no' when it is necessary, and say it with conviction, you will not only recover your power, but you will also reclaim your right to life, happiness, purpose, and love.

2. Put an end to the "I'll save you" game.

I've always admired Buddha's quote:

"We are the only ones who can save ourselves." No one can and no one should. We must take the journey ourselves." The Buddha

You may believe you've come to save people and guide them back on track. But that is not 'your' job. That is 'their' responsibility!

Each person has his or her own inherent guidance and heavenly power. And it is up to them to figure out their path and why they are in this world.

No matter how tempting it is to put yourself in the role of 'the savior' and hand over your power to them, you must recognize that you are not here to save anyone.

You're also not here to persuade individuals that they deserve a better life. You've come to travel your own path and live your own life. And if you can inspire others to do the same, that's fantastic. If not, there is nothing that can be done.

3. Reclaim your power by separating yourself from poisonous people.

I know you're a wonderful person who has difficulty stepping away. However, entertaining people who physically take the life out of you will leave you feeling helpless, confused, and deprived of crucial vitality.

It is your life to live. You also have the right to leave.

You have the right to set healthy limits and care for yourself. So, please, reclaim your authority and learn to do what is best for you.

4. Regain control by letting go of blame.

I know you believe you have the right to blame the past, your parents, your partner, your family, the government, or whoever harmed you for all of the terrible and toxic feelings that have been stored in your body for so long. And you could be correct.

But guess what? It no longer makes a difference.

Do you understand why?

Because holding onto blame is one of the most destructive things you can do. And the longer you hold on to it, the weaker you will feel, making it more difficult for you to reclaim your power and be true to yourself. It's simply not worth holding on to. Allow it to go.

5. Have faith in yourself

You are considerably more powerful than you realize and far more tough than you realize. And you must begin to consider yourself as such.

You must begin to trust yourself again not when things will improve, not when you will gain confidence, not when the Sun will shine, but now!

6. Be brave enough to walk alone.

There will be times in your life when you will be asked to embark on an adventure into the unknown. There will be times when no one will be there to grasp your hand and walk alongside you.

When that happens, I want you to remember that you have nothing to be afraid of. Your Soul is present to assist you.

To paraphrase the Psalmist, "Even though I walk through the darkest valley, I will fear no evil, for you are with me; your rod and your staff, they comfort me." Psalm 23:4

If you seek within and pray for strength, knowledge, courage, and confidence, you will receive them. So don't worry.

You are never alone, even if you are walking through the darkest valley.

7. Reclaim your authority.

Reclaim your power by doing the things you used to enjoy but stopped doing; by saying 'no' when it is necessary; and by no longer viewing yourself as little, weak, and helpless.

Reclaim your power by seeing yourself as the beautiful, strong, courageous being you were born to be.

And by realizing that it is your life to live and your power to keep.

You are not required to give it to anyone.

Take your power back from wherever you left it, and promise yourself that you will never give it to anyone else again.

Chapter 8

love for oneself

It may take time to love oneself, but it is achievable for everyone. Self-love entails having faith, confidence, and pride in oneself and one's abilities.

Setting boundaries, being mindful, and removing toxic people from your life are all part of practicing self-love.

Seek out a therapist, journal, and listen to affirmations to help you develop self-love.

You only have one person with whom you spend every second of every day of your life. Fostering a loving connection with yourself might be a lengthy and difficult process, but it will allow for more enjoyment and freedom.

What exactly is self-love?

Self-love is defined as a sense of trust, confidence, and pride in oneself and one's skills.

Self-love allows you to enjoy the good times in life while also believing in your ability to handle the bad.

Self-love can be tough to achieve because of internalized thoughts that you're not good enough, or feelings of guilt about putting your needs first.

"Developing self-love can take time, patience, and practice, but self-love is deserved and achievable by all." Here are six methods for practicing self-love.

Here's all you need to know about self-love.

1. Take care of yourself.
Self-care is defined as everything you do to improve your physical, mental, or emotional wellness.

There are numerous ways to practice self-care, including:

•Watching a movie or a television show
•Making a dinner
•Take part in a game.

•Taking a walk

•You should clean your apartment.

•Brushing and flossing your teeth

•Exercising

2. Practice mindfulness

Mindfulness is being aware of what you are sensing and feeling in the present moment without passing judgment. By focusing on the now, mindfulness attempts to guide you away from the past or future.

"Being able to listen to your body and mind and be aware of your needs is the best thing that can be done for you specifically," Annie M. Henderson, a trained professional life coach and licensed professional counselor, says.

What the research says: According to a major 2015 evaluation, mindfulness-based therapies enhanced participants' self-esteem.

Mindfulness can be practiced in a variety of ways, including:

•Meditation

•Count your breaths or take big breaths

•Exercising your feet

•Pay attention to your five senses, such as what you smell, hear, and feel.

3. Examine negative thoughts
When you have a thought that says, "I'm not worthy" or "I can't do this," challenge it.

What causes you to feel this way, and how can you change your viewpoint to focus on your accomplishments?

Also, consider how external variables are influencing your perception of oneself.

"Sometimes you're underperforming at work, but sometimes their expectations are exploitative," Daramus goes on to remark. "Sometimes you're 'not there for a friend or significant other, but sometimes their needs are unreasonable."

4. Establish limits

Setting physical and emotional boundaries gives you power over how you treat yourself and others, both of which are necessary for self-love. It allows you to prioritize your demands and express them verbally.

Setting limits can take the form of:

•Learning to say "no" without feeling guilty

•Making a decision regardless of what others think of you

•Defending yourself and your needs

•Your boundaries may shift over time, and setting new ones does not necessitate an apology.

5. Do not compare yourself to others.

It's way too simple to see an idealized image of other people's lives and successes thanks to social media. Comparing oneself to someone else's carefully maintained online presence can be harmful to self-love.

"Remember that social media is an extreme version of the public persona or mask folks project, but only represents a sliver of the challenges, problems, and difficulties that color individuals' lives," Romanoff said.

What the research says: According to a 2018 study, students who used social media to compare themselves and seek positive feedback from peers were more likely to develop symptoms of sadness and seek reassurance excessively offline.

6. Get rid of harmful people in your life.
A toxic individual might make it difficult to cultivate self-love. While you can attain self-love on your own, it is much easier when you are surrounded by positive affirmations and respect.

According to Henderson, harmful characteristics may include:

•Being averse to or afraid of your own progress

•Having only bad things to say

•Ignoring your thoughts

•Ignoring your limits

•After spending time together, you will be fatigued.

•After speaking with someone, ask yourself, "Do I feel better or worse than I did before the conversation began?"

How do you cultivate self-love?

There are numerous approaches to developing self-love, and one ideal for each individual will differ.

"While waking up at 5 AM, meditation, and journaling might really give someone a sense of self-love, it could be dancing, running, or talking to a life coach or therapist," Henderson said. "Consistency is key when it comes to self-love and finding something that works for you."

Here are a few ways to try for increasing self-love

•Seek assistance

According to research, therapists can assist in the development of self-love and self-esteem. They can gently guide you to understand the source of your insecurities and then help you overcome them. "A therapist can also check for underlying problems, like depression, anxiety, or trauma," Daramus said.

•Practice self-love meditation

A self-love meditation, like mindfulness, includes sitting with yourself and inspiring sentiments of love and kindness towards yourself.

Journal. Writing can improve your sense of well-being by allowing you to become more aware of your emotions, what you're proud of, characteristics of yourself you like, and steps you're taking to achieve your goals.

•Pay attention to affirmations

Affirmations are phrases you can say to yourself when your feelings of self-love are wavering or need a boost. Affirmations can include things like "I am worthy" or "I am loved." Affirmation applications and notebooks are available to help you get started.

•Insider knowledge

Self-love is an ongoing process with ups and downs. Self-love can be practiced and developed on your own or with the assistance of a mental health professional. Listening to your needs, challenging negative beliefs, and removing individuals from your life who bring you down are all examples of self-love.

Chapter 9

The question is whether to go or stay

When examining this question, many people become stuck. They may feel strongly one way in the morning and strongly the opposite way by the time they go to bed. Many persons who are going through the legal procedure express remorse over their decision and worry that it is too late to reverse things.

Finally, the decision is yours (you know what is best for you and your position); yet, given the serious ramifications, it is prudent to take your time and truly tap into your wisdom to lead you. These questions are designed to assist you in making the best decision for you (and future you).

1. How secure is your relationship?

Abuse in relationships can take many different forms. Physical abuse is commonly known as one spouse (or both) beating, kicking, slapping, or otherwise physically injuring or threatening the other. Other forms of abuse may be more difficult to detect, yet they can be just as (or even more) harmful.

One spouse can attempt to exercise power and control over another through emotional, sexual, financial, psychological, and cultural/identity abuse. Patterns of any or all of these behaviors can signal that a relationship is unsafe, and it may be necessary to seek help to either dramatically change the relationship or leave.

Relationships built on trust, caring for one another, and respect, on the other hand, achieve a fundamental degree of safety on which to build.

All of the other questions in this post presuppose that your relationship is secure.

2. Does your partner know you're thinking about terminating the relationship?

Sometimes one partner will oscillate between wanting to stay and wanting to leave for months or years before making a decision, and their spouse may be completely unaware that they are unhappy. However, the spouse may notice

little differences and develop self-protective habits, further damaging the connection.

Speaking to your partner and telling them how you're feeling can be daunting, but not speaking to them (some people don't even mention how they're feeling in couples therapy) can leave the fundamental issues unsolved.

3. Have you tried everything to save your relationship?

The painful feelings that arise during a couple's quarrel are quite potent. People's anger, fear, and hurt can lead to desperate attempts to end the pain, even if it means leaving the relationship early. However, most people have fewer regrets when they put in the effort to rescue their relationship before realizing it isn't salvageable.

70% of couples who receive treatment benefit from couples therapy! A skilled couples therapist with specific training on how to assist couples work through their problems can help relationships, even those on the verge of divorce, survive and thrive.

4. Are you aware of how you may be contributing to the relationship's difficulties?

Except in violent relationships, both spouses are frequently responsible for the patterns that emerge. Childhood experiences and other relationships can have an impact on how people present themselves in romantic relationships. Although looking closely at your own habits might be difficult or frightening, evaluating how your ideas, emotions, and behaviors may be part of a cycle that affects your relationship may provide some clarity as to which next step is best for you.

Furthermore,

Whether you stay or leave your relationship, having a careful look at yourself can be beneficial.

5. How will either decision affect you, your children, your relationship, your money, your traditions, and your way of life, and are you prepared to deal with the consequences?

Many people make successful decisions when they investigate as many facets of the decision as feasible. Consider things like, "What will our children learn about relationships by watching us stay together (or separate)?" "Do I have a plan to support myself when I'm on my own?"

"Am I ready to let go of my partner physically, mentally, emotionally, and spiritually?" Questions about the long-term consequences of your decision may assist you in determining whether your decision to end the relationship is a reaction to a short-term problem or a decision based on self-awareness and serious thinking.

6. Is your decision motivated by fear or by a more optimistic outlook for the future?

Some people approach the choice to end a relationship with trepidation. "What if no one else ever loves me the way my partner does?" "What if we can never figure out how to stop arguing so much?" Others approach the decision with a vision of a better future in mind.

"What would my life look like if I could invest the time and energy I am spending on fighting with my partner into my own self-development?" "What might happen if both of us commit to working on our relationship as a team?" In a circumstance as important as quitting a relationship, fear-based thinking is a normal response.

However, it may not result in the greatest decisions. If your safety is not an issue, consider deferring your decision until you can approach it with a forward-thinking perspective.

You may be able to reach this point on your own, or you may benefit from the assistance of a therapist. This way of thinking may help you make the finest decision for your future.

7. What information does your body have regarding your decision for you?

Thoughts can vary and move from one moment to the next, while physical reactions are more steady. What occurs in your body when you envisage

yourself five years from now with your partner? Do you have a tightness in your chest, a weight in your stomach, or an upper lip curl? Sensations like this could be a clue that it's time to go.

Or do you feel a sensation of expansion, a relaxing of your movements, or a pleasant feeling stretching across your chest? These body sensations may signal that you are going through difficult times, but that the foundation of your relationship is still intact.

Paying attention to your physiological sensations can provide valuable information about which decision is best for you.

Choosing whether to stay or leave a relationship can be a painful experience. It is common to experience conflict and confusion, anger and sadness, excitement and depression all in the same day.
Taking the time to explore all choices and obtaining the necessary support (whether from a journal, friends and family, or a therapist) can make the process smoother and result in fewer "What ifs?" and regrets down the road.

Chapter 10

Hello and welcome to the rest of your life. It is possible to recover from an abusive relationship.

Here are some useful steps for healing while still prioritizing your well-being.

You've already taken one of the most critical stages in the process if you've recently left an abusive relationship.

Learning how to recover and care for yourself after a breakup might help you navigate the following steps.

Common experiences in the aftermath of an abusive relationship
Abuse can take various forms, including settings and relationships.

•emotional

•physical

•verbal

•sexual

•spiritual

•financial (e.g., regulating joint finances, limiting access to funds)

•Reproductive coercion (e.g., breaking condoms, interfering with access to birth control)

•Digital (e.g., stalking, demanding passwords or phone access)

When recovering from an abusive relationship, a wide range of emotional feelings may surface, many of which are valid.

Depending on the circumstances, you may have some of the following thoughts or feelings:

•you miss your ex

•loneliness or isolation

•considering returning to the relationship

•feeling unsure or incapable of making judgments on your own

•Anxiety or depression symptoms

•finding it challenging to feel self-sufficient

•a persistent fear or sense of danger

•Post-traumatic stress disorder (PTSD) symptoms

You may also have good feelings. "Sometimes a survivor can feel a sense of freedom, as if a weight has been lifted off their shoulders." Other days, you may be overcome with melancholy and anxiety, and you may question everything," she continues.

"All of these feelings, from feeling free and empowered to feeling lonely and missing your ex, are entirely natural."

How long might it take to heal?
"Healing isn't always the first thing that comes to mind when someone quits an abusive relationship. "It's survival," adds Gross.

There is no established time schedule for recovery because each survivor's experience is unique.

"But what is there is the possibility to get to a place where you know, understand, and can respond appropriately to your triggers," she said.

How to Get Over an Abusive Relationship

Although the healing process is not a straight line, there are methods to find solace and support along the road.

Make a safety plan (if you haven't done so already).

According to Gross, safety planning can provide you with a sense of control and protection: "You can add responses for different circumstances, such as seeing [your ex] in public or if they contact you on social media."

"Make your safety and security the top priority post-breakup, so you can focus on yourself and your healing journey," Onyema adds in a press release.

Establish boundaries

Setting boundaries after a relationship is as crucial as setting them during it.

"Make sure you and your ex are on the same page in terms of communication and behavior," she goes on to add.

"And; if you're not, and you very well may not remember that your needs and boundaries are important."

Be forthright in stating them and strong in your right to the time and space you require."

Consider setting digital limits, such as blocking your ex or taking a sabbatical from social media.

Knowing that your partner doesn't have access to you on social media can provide the distance you might need to move through healing at your own pace, making self-care and self-love a priority.

Self-care and self-love is vital because without them, survivors can find themselves in another abusive relationship. Respect your thoughts and feelings as they arise.
"Make the most of your newfound time by focusing on activities that will boost your confidence and help you regain emotional balance." "You've earned it,"

Affirmations for healing should be repeated several times.
continual to remind yourself that the abuse was never your fault: "Set an alarm on your phone or write it on a Post-It note and do it."
"It can be hard not to look back on your past relationship with rose-colored glasses, or you may feel like you miss your ex-partner,

but keep in mind that you're strong, and you'll get through it, Remember that everyone including you deserves a healthy relationship where they feel loved, respected, and valued.

Learn more about abuse.

Learning about abuse, no matter where you are in your journey, might help you avoid similar circumstances in the future.

"When everyone has a better understanding and knowledge of how intimate partner violence works, we will be able to remove the stigma and provide the necessary support and services to survivors and perpetrators."

Create a robust support system.

You are not required to accomplish this alone. During the recovery process, receiving support can help you feel stronger and more connected.

A great support system can include family, friends, a therapist, coach, personal trainer, [and] support group, Someone in an abusive relationship is frequently isolated from friends and family.

"It's good to see them again." [They] can provide emotional support, boost your self-esteem, and counteract some of the doubts or negative feelings we may have about ourselves following a breakup."

Ask for assistance.
Consider consulting with a therapist or other mental health professional. Therapy can teach you useful coping strategies after an abusive relationship and provide additional support during the recovery process.

Other resources for help are available, including:

•hotlines for domestic violence

•groups such as One Love

•survivor events and programs

•joining support groups to connect with other survivors

"Don't let shame or embarrassment keep you from getting your needs met," advises Gross, who encourages utilizing all available resources.

Conclusion

Narcissistic personality disorder dominates a person's daily thought processes and actions, affecting their relationships. Narcissists project their formative trauma onto those around them, transmitting lifetime fears and tension.

Reality can be a daily battle for their partner and families. The daily challenges frequently have long-term consequences, including psychiatric illnesses.

Marriages and families can be ruined, even if they appear charming from the outside. The transmission of low self-esteem generates a toxic family that appears to be irreparable and is difficult to forgive.

The partner's life altered the moment they met the narcissistic person, and their children have never known anything other than walking on eggshells. It is tough for all family members to comprehend being deprived of rest and happiness.

The source of unacknowledged, daily anxiety is a sensitive matter that should be handled by a specialist. Although it may appear unlikely, rehabilitation is feasible, and all family members can improve their mental health.

Marriage partners and families must be willing to accept internal flaws and collaborate to create a better family dynamic. Therapists will use their knowledge and resources to treat the narcissistic people and others they have impacted the most efficiently.
Individuals should not necessarily expect a good conclusion when it comes to couples therapy. If they stick with the therapy for a long time, they should expect to learn about each partner's deeper layers of daily fears and concerns.

Divorce is sometimes the only option, yet it is still a type of therapy. Families can also seek therapy or other rehabilitation programs to identify long-term psychological impacts.

In every treatment situation, the therapist attempts to uncover the source of the issue and how the couple/family may work together to improve relationships.

It may appear impossible to forgive the cause of one's psychiatric issues, but narcissists are victims of their own upbringing. Unfortunately, mental illnesses are a vicious cycle influenced by both nature and nurture.

Attending treatment and believing in the potential of recovery can help to break the cycle and lay the groundwork for future families. Those suffering from narcissistic personality disorder deserve a second chance, and families can recover from the pain caused by these people.

Consider the United States' underwhelming jail sector. Internal jail arrangements do not successfully promote rehabilitation, which is why more than half of individuals who enter the system are destined to re-enter.

This is a shocking statistic, and many people find it impossible to sympathize with those who break the law and ruin people's lives. However, they often forget why those people were in that predicament and belittle their own privilege.

Similarly, narcissists have succumbed to the harmful reality of their childhood. They will re-enter their own jail system of internal fights and the devastation of loved ones if adequate rehabilitation is not provided.